CHALLENGING THE CULTURE OF CORRUPTION

Game-Changing Reform For Illinois

Patrick M. Collins

acta
PUBLICATIONS

CHALLENGING THE CULTURE OF CORRUPTION
Game-Changing Reform for Illinois

by Patrick M. Collins

Edited by Gregory F. Augustine Pierce
Cover design by Tom A. Wright
Text design and typesetting by Complete Communications, Inc.

Published by ACTA Publications, 5559 W. Howard Street, Skokie, IL 60077-2621, (800) 397-2282, www.actapublications.com

Library of Congress Catalog number: 2009944225
ISBN: 978-0-87946-424-0
Printed in Illinois by Total Printing Systems

Year: 15 14 13 12 11 10
Printing: 8 7 6 5 4 3 2 First

 Text printed on 30% post-consumer recycled paper.

Contents

This book is dedicated to my wife and partner Helena, and our wonderful children, Luke, Gabrielle, Nicola, and Quinn. You all are the inspiration for anything good that I will ever do.

I also write this book in thoughtful memory of Benjamin, Joseph, Samuel, Hank, Elizabeth, and Peter Willis. I never met you, but I will always remember each of you and your parents' incredible humanity and dignity in the face of unimaginable grief.

100% of any royalties received from this book will be donated to not-for-profit reform groups dedicated to challenging the culture of corruption in Illinois and other charitable organizations.

Introduction: The Challenge

It was a day I will never forget: March 8, 2006. During the closing arguments to the jury in the six-month criminal corruption trial of former Illinois Governor George Ryan, his highly skilled lawyer, Dan Webb, had just spent seven hours dissecting the evidence our team presented to the jury. We had offered a mountain of evidence of pay-to-play political corruption, Illinois style: the steering of lucrative contracts and sweetheart leases to personal friends and campaign donors; the use and theft of government resources for campaign purposes; the cover-up of the licenses-for-bribes scandal that had fueled Ryan's political ambitions; and Ryan's lying to the FBI. As Webb finished with an emotional plea for the jury to acquit Ryan and send him home, a hush came over the courtroom gallery and the Court announced a break.

As our prosecution team walked past the gallery out of the courtroom to prepare for our final argument, I felt someone grab my arm. I turned and saw a red-faced Scott Willis, a victim of Illinois' culture of corruption and the Ryan Administration's licenses-for-bribes cover-up. As I turned toward Scott, who had witnessed Webb's blistering attack on our evidence from the gallery, he asked in a very uncertain tone, "Are we still okay?" Scott wanted to know whether I thought the evidence we had presented would overcome the skillful arguments made on Ryan's behalf. The truthful response was that I had no clue, as Webb had been quite effective at poking holes in our case. But I didn't have the heart to say that to Scott, so I simply mumbled something unintelligible and told him we had a lot of work to do to prepare our final argument to the jury the next day.

Motivated in no small measure by Scott's watchful presence, our team spent most of the night crafting our response. Hours later, we had our opportunity to talk directly to the jurors one last time about the years of corruption that had stained our state. The jury then began deliberating, and two weeks later they found Ryan guilty on each and every count of a wide-ranging corruption indictment. I took no personal solace in the fact that another disgraced governor of our great state was headed to jail.

In many respects, the jury's decision made in a federal courtroom in March of 2006 began back on November 8, 1994. On that day, George Ryan was re-elected as Secretary of State for Illinois. Later that same day, Scott Willis, an Illinois resident who had voted for Ryan that morning, and his family were the victims of a fatal traffic incident caused by a truck driver who should not have been on the road. Over a decade later, these two seemingly unrelated events would be linked together in that federal courtroom in Ryan's criminal trial. The connection: Illinois' culture of corruption.

Fast forward to December 9, 2008. Only one year after Ryan was sent to prison, his successor, Governor Rod Blagojevich, was awakened by federal agents who arrested him and took him into custody. The arrest led to the impeachment of Blagojevich and installation of his successor, Lt. Governor Pat Quinn. In the aftermath of Blagojevich's arrest, there was a loud outcry from public officials demanding that we address Illinois' integrity crisis. The target: the culture of corruption.

Separated by fourteen years, these two sequences shaped my personal views of Illinois' political culture. In the earlier sequence, it was part of my job to expose corruption in criminal cases in federal courtrooms. In the later sequence, as Quinn's selection to lead a reform effort, it became part of my job to propose positive reforms to our state's corruption problems.

What we have experienced in Illinois over the last decade is unprecedented. In the last five years alone, successive governors—representing both major political parties—and those in their respective inner circles, have been charged with serious public corruption crimes. Outside the governor's mansion, at the city, county, and state level, investigative reporters and federal prosecutors have revealed all-too-frequent political scandals and breaches of the public trust. Even with the media casting an intense spotlight and prosecutors aggressively pursuing criminal cases, the steady drumbeat of corruption revelations seems to continue unabated.

Coupled with the widespread effects of this culture of corruption, we also have a dysfunctional democracy in which the decisions made and agendas set by our government often ignore or diverge from the most important issues that affect citizens across the state. The result is that our government leaders continue to delay and avoid important public policy decisions without consequence. While I don't know whether the culture of corruption has directly caused this dysfunctional democracy, I do believe the two are related. More importantly, this dual problem serves a one-two punch on Illinois citizens and defines our current political life.

Given this track record, what should be done to change our political culture in Illinois?

This book is my small contribution to that important question. While I believe I have had a unique opportunity to observe the problems that have resulted from this culture, I do not pretend to have all the answers. Based on my experiences, however, I do have concrete thoughts on where we should currently wage the battle to change Illinois. My hope is that this book, along with other ongoing efforts of citizens committed to reform, will help continue an important dialogue with Illinois citizens and policy makers about how to remove the painful and expensive stain of corruption we all have endured.

This book is also a call to action to my fellow citizens of the "Land of Lincoln." In order to achieve a long-term solution to this problem, we cannot expect that any one politician or singular change in the law will change the game or the attitudes of its players. Rather, we need a dynamic, long-term strategy driven by individuals, institutions, and dedicated organizations who will challenge the culture of corruption that has made our state the laughingstock of the nation.

How long will it take to reverse our state's corruption course? During my recent work as the chair of the Illinois Reform Commission (IRC), I received many calls, emails and letters from members of the public. One person, an organizational expert, called me to volunteer his thoughts on what it would take to change Illinois' culture of corruption. He said something that has stayed with me: As long as it has taken the culture of corruption to take root in Illinois, he offered, that is how long it will take to rid the corruption mentality from our state. If he is right, it means we are in for a long journey back to a high-functioning political system. Yet, it is a journey that should begin with several significant steps.

And how far we get toward achieving our reform objectives will depend on whether enough of us who have been on the sidelines will take ownership of our government in ways we have not done before. If not us, then who will take on this mission? If not now, then when will we begin to accomplish it? Yes, the stakes are quite high, but this is not a story of gloom and doom. After all, we are the state that has provided transformative national figures from Lincoln to Reagan to Obama. We have sparked movements in civil liberties, women's rights, and racial and social justice. We can succeed.

As a state, we are better than this, but we need your help—now and tomorrow—to reverse the culture of corruption and become a model for the nation on how a healthy democracy should work.

Patrick Collins
Chicago, Illinois
January, 2010

I. My Education in the Culture of Corruption

As a federal prosecutor working public corruption cases in Illinois for over a decade, I received a unique education in Illinois' culture of corruption. The education actually began in 1991, when I was an impressionable law student serving as an intern in the United States Attorney's office in Chicago. I was working in the office library late one afternoon when Tom Durkin, the number two prosecutor in the office, whom I had never met, came into the library looking for intern help on one of his cases. Luckily for me, I was the only intern there. He asked me if I would be willing to help his prosecution team on a recently indicted public corruption case. I jumped at the chance. What he didn't say—and what I soon found out—is that the case was no ordinary case. It was a high-profile case involving a prominent Democratic Cook County judge, David Shields, who was accused of taking a cash bribe to fix a civil case pending before him. For the next several months, I assisted the prosecutors in any way I could. In so doing, I had a front-row seat in the unique theater of Illinois political corruption.

After my internship was over and I watched the case proceed to trial, where a jury found Judge Shields guilty of taking the bribe, a question nagged at me: How was it possible that—only a few years after the highly-publicized cases of Operation Greylord, where scores of Cook County judges and court personnel were convicted of taking bribes and hauled off to jail—a judge in the same Cook County system could be involved in the same sort of crime? Hadn't everyone in the judicial system gotten the message?

The experience of the Shields case enhanced my desire to seek a position at the U.S. Attorney's office after graduating law school. In 1995, four years after graduating, that opportunity finally came. Within weeks of my starting as an Assistant United States Attorney, fate would smile upon me again when my direct supervisor approached me and asked me

14

if I wanted to assist Scott Levine, a senior corruption prosecutor, on another high-profile case—this one involving allegations of corruption at the Cook County Sheriff's office. In that investigation, involving Republican Undersheriff James Dvorak, a number of high-ranking officials were charged with operating a fraudulent hiring and ghost-payrolling operation within the Sheriff's department. The notion that such a criminal scheme could be run by high-ranking officials in a law enforcement department was, like the result of the Shields case, mindboggling to me.

While these first two corruption investigations made a significant impact on me, the most memorable lessons began in the summer of 1998.

At that time, I was a relatively inexperienced prosecutor leading my first major public corruption investigation, code-named Operation Safe Road. Our investigative team, led by the FBI, received information that truck driving applicants were paying cash bribes of $1,000 or more to Illinois Secretary of State George Ryan's office managers in order to get passed on the license exams. Once the licenses were obtained, these individuals drove large semis across Illinois and throughout the nation. Given that many were unqualified to be driving, the potential harmful effects on public safety were obvious. We knew we had to be aggressive to expose the wrongdoing.

That summer, lead FBI agent Ken Samuel called me with an important development. A person cooperating with the FBI agreed to make an introduction of an undercover agent posing as an unqualified truck driving applicant to the corrupt ring of individuals who were bribing Secretary of State employees. After we confirmed that this corruption was indeed ongoing, we brought this information to a federal judge to request authority to obtain wiretaps—that is, the authority to secretly record the phone conversations of those involved. A primary purpose of these wiretaps was to obtain evidence as to how extensive the illegal acts were.

As we began to record secretly the conversations involving Ryan's employees in the Secretary of State's office, we began hearing some of the reasons—that is, the motive—why these relatively low-level employees were engaged in these crimes. In some of the calls, the employees talked cryptically about how they were using this bribe money to meet their quota of political fundraising tickets. As we later learned, these employees, many of whom made less than $40,000 per year, were expected to sell political fundraising tickets to support the Ryan political campaign. For some, they were given over $10,000 in tickets per year to sell. So, without legitimate means to meet these excessive "quotas," they sold the truck licenses and, in the process, their integrity. As we moved forward in the investigation, we saw that this was not an isolated group of employees. Rather, dozens of Secretary of State employees across the Chicagoland area were selling licenses for bribes, and hundreds of thousands of dollars in bribe proceeds were being directed to the Ryan political campaign. Worst of all, we traced nine fatalities to truck drivers who had illegally obtained their licenses. This was a tangible cost of corruption.

This was not an isolated group of employees selling licenses for bribes.

A critical question for our investigative team was how far and wide did this licenses-for-bribes corruption go? In the fall of 1998, George Ryan had been promoted by the voters of Illinois to governor, our state's highest office, but Operation Safe Road didn't stop because Ryan was elected governor. Having seen that this licenses-for-bribes misconduct was widespread within Ryan's Secretary of State office, we followed the evidence and began to ask some investigative questions about the higher-ups: What did they know and when did they know it?

We caught some key breaks in the investigation by talking to former Secretary of State investigators whose job it had been to investigate employee misconduct for that office. Several of them told us that in the early 1990s they had been looking quite closely at these same licenses-for-bribes issues, including this fundraising ticket motive that we had heard on our 1998 wiretaps. One tragic incident—and the ensuing internal investigation—was particularly memorable for them.

---

*One tragic incident
—and the ensuing internal investigation—
was particularly memorable for them.*

Back to the fateful day, November 8, 1994. A van carrying Scott and Janet Willis and their six children was heading up the expressway into Wisconsin. The truck immediately in front of them was driven by a man named Ricardo Guzman. Unbeknownst to Scott and Janet Willis, Guzman had paid cash to get his truck license from one of those prolific ticket-selling supervisors at the Secretary of State's office. As a result, Guzman was driving on a fraudulent license and should not have been on the road that day. After the Willis van passed into Wisconsin, a metal piece that had been dangling from the Guzman truck dropped from his truck onto the road. (Efforts by other motorists to warn Guzman about the precarious condition of his truck went unheeded or unnoticed.) The metal object punctured the gas tank of the Willis van. Six of the Willis children died in the ensuing crash and explosion. Scott and Janet were badly burned. While Scott and Janet would physically recover, their lives had been tragically and irreparably changed.

Their lives had been tragically and irreparably changed.

A conscientious Secretary of State investigator by the name of Russ Sonneveld saw the news report of this deadly incident. In 1993 and 1994, Sonneveld and his partner, Ed Hammer, had been investigating licenses-for-bribes activities, including allegations that sales of Ryan campaign fundraising tickets were the motive behind some of the illegal activity. Sonneveld immediately began to investigate by pulling Guzman's license application. Sonneveld recognized the name of the Secretary of State employee who had signed off on Guzman's paperwork as a prolific Ryan ticket seller. His suspicions were aroused, and he went to his boss and asked for permission to talk to Guzman to see how he had secured his Illinois license. Sonneveld's boss, George Ryan's close friend Dean Bauer, told him not to pursue the matter. Bauer told Sonneveld that the Guzman incident happened in Wisconsin and thus was of no relevance to Illinois or Ryan's office. Citing Guzman's Illinois license, Sonneveld protested, but ultimately Bauer prevailed and the investigation stalled.

Five years later, in the midst of our Operation Safe Road investigation, I received a call from Don Strom, Bauer's successor for the new Secretary of State's administration. During a law enforcement search for records in the bowels of the Secretary of State's office, the agents had found a "smoking gun" memo from Bauer describing the Guzman incident. The memo announced that Bauer would be handling the Guzman investigation personally. Yet this Bauer memo was dated the same day he told Sonneveld not to pursue the case, an order that effectively killed the investigation. To us, the memo seemed to tell the story of a cover-up: Bauer wanted to ensure that nothing was done on the Guzman investigation, and indeed, we later discovered, nothing was ever done. Even though it was Bauer's job to investigate, the

Ryan Administration never gave the Willis family the investigation they deserved. The culture of corruption lived on.

A few months later, lead FBI agent Ray Ruebenson came upon a second "smoking gun" document: a secret December 1994 memo written by Ryan's chief of staff, Scott Fawell. Fawell recommended to Ryan that "trouble maker" internal investigators—guys like Sonneveld and Hammer—be fired. The rationale Fawell cited to Ryan was that the investigators were too eagerly probing Ryan's campaign's friends and asking too many questions about political fundraising tickets. Of course, that's precisely what the investigators were doing, because of the unholy alliance between the licensing process and political fundraising that benefitted Ryan.

Rather than separate the licensing process from fundraising, Ryan chose to accept Fawell's recommendation to gut the investigative office. Sonneveld and Hammer were effectively fired, and meaningful investigations into the licenses-for-bribes scandal were stopped dead in their tracks.

Of course, we were never supposed to see this Fawell memo, as some of those in Ryan's inner circle tried to shred documents and destroy computer disks containing damaging information in order to keep the records from us. But due to the great work of the agents, we retrieved the information, and the documents told a tale of an office motivated primarily by campaign contributions and political ambition.

The documents told a tale of an office motivated primarily by campaign contributions and political ambition.

With the licenses-for-bribes evidence pointing to participation by high-ranking officials in the Secretary of State's office, it seemed that this case was no longer about a "few bad apples" at the lower levels of the Secretary of State's office. This appeared to be a more systematic and widespread corruption scheme in which bribe proceeds were used to fuel Ryan's political ambitions. When questions were asked about the fundraising apparatus, the people asking the questions were fired. At the highest levels of the office, coordinated efforts were made to shred, destroy, and hide evidence. The governor himself later chose to lie to federal investigators about his knowledge of licenses-for-bribes investigations, as well as his role in profiting from governmental decisions he made.

As key details of the scandal had yet to be discovered by the time of the November 1998 gubernatorial election, Ryan was rewarded by the citizens of Illinois with the highest office in the state. The culture of corruption continued to thrive.

But federal investigators continued their work. In 2003, after dozens and dozens of individuals were charged and convicted as part of Operation Safe Road, George Ryan himself was then indicted for widespread corruption, including actions he took in gutting the Inspector General's office in 1994, just as his internal investigators were asking hard questions about the unfolding licenses-for-bribes scandal.

Notably, the licenses-for-bribes allegations were but a small part of the allegations against Ryan. In general, the Ryan indictment alleged a pay-to-play scheme where his office's leases, lucrative contracts, and even low-digit or "vanity" license plates were put up for sale to personal friends and campaign contributors. In one case, Ryan personally steered an above-market lease in South Holland, Illinois, to a friend who treated him to a freebie Jamaican vacation every year; in another, he steered a lucrative lease in Joliet, Illinois, to another long-time friend who was providing Ryan and his family with loans, gifts, and other financial benefits. All the while, Ryan's chief of staff, Scott Fawell, kept score of what was being given to whom in a 500-page master list, which list ultimately gave us the roadmap of the Ryan Administration's corruption.

A public trial then ensued in which the sordid details of this pay-to-play government were revealed. Ryan's ultimate conviction at trial on all charges in March of 2006 symbolized a government that had lost its way: a corrupt office fueled by political ambition and condoned by the very people who had been elected and appointed to protect the public trust. Our state's highest official, George Ryan, was sent to jail. The very real and human costs of corruption—as personified by victims like Scott and Janet Willis—could not be ignored.

In 2002, against the backdrop of Ryan's impending indictment, a man named Rod Blagojevich capitalized on the voter's disgust with the Ryan Administration's corruption and won the highest office in the land. Yet Blagojevich apparently paid little heed to the Ryan criminal justice lesson. According to the allegations of the next major federal probe in Illinois, dubbed Operation Board Games, Blagojevich took the Ryan pay-to-play corruption playbook to a new level. Most amazing of all, he allegedly committed these corrupt acts just as Ryan's case publicly played out before him and all of Illinois.

So while the name of the federal corruption probe and the alleged wrongdoers had changed, the culture of corruption had not. In fact, based on the public allegations, things got worse and the corruption even more brazen. On December 9, 2008, in an early morning law enforcement action, Blagojevich was arrested and the torch of institutional corruption in Illinois was officially passed.

> *While the name of the federal corruption probe and the alleged wrongdoers had changed, the culture of corruption had not.*

While Operation Safe Road was my most memorable work experience, it was not my only point of reference. For almost ten years, I worked alongside dedicated federal prosecutors and law enforcement agents who reviewed a steady stream of allegations of corruption at the city, county, and state level.

As I mentioned earlier, the first extensive corruption investigation I was involved in after I earned my law degree was an inquiry into a corrupt scheme directed by James Dvorak, the number two official at the Cook County Sheriff's office. Dvorak and a number of others were convicted of falsifying test scores on merit applications and hiring ghost payrollers to the Sheriff's payroll. The principal motive was to help political friends and campaign contributors obtain the benefits of Sheriff's office employment. For some, they were given bogus jobs by higher-ups merely so they could have guns and badges.

In addition, there was a multi-year scandal involving high-ranking officials at the City of Chicago. In this investigation, dubbed "Hired Truck," over 40 individuals were convicted of various schemes involving a $40 million per year truck-outsourcing program in the city's largest operating departments. Department officials awarded lucrative trucking contracts in return for cash, campaign contributions, and other financial benefits. There was little or no bidding process involved in the award of these contracts, and not surprisingly, contract prices were often inflated and the work substandard. But that wasn't all. Many of the same players also were involved in a related patronage fraud scheme, whereby the hiring process for city jobs and promotions was rigged and falsified to help the connected and clouted. The victims were the many hard-working people who deserved the jobs and promotions, as well as the taxpayers who paid for a process that awarded clout over merit.

In an egregious case that demonstrated the potentially tragic consequences of this "run-of-the-mill"

corruption, an unqualified 19-year-old was fraudulently awarded a coveted position as a building inspector. Building inspectors had the important job of
ensuring that the city's buildings were maintained
in accordance with safety regulations. The possible
consequences of hiring unqualified buildings inspectors were brought to mind after two back-to-back,
highly publicized fatal incidents in Chicago (a night-
club stampede and a porch collapse). In both cases,
public attention was brought to the importance
of having high-functioning inspectors. While the
19-year-old had absolutely no connection to the two
fatal incidents, his hiring was symptomatic of the
broken system. The concern that human tragedies
could result from a corrupt hiring system could no
longer be ignored.

Yet it seemed that the allegations never stopped
coming in the door, and worst of all, as exhibited by
the Blagojevich allegations, the deterrent message
sent by high-profile prosecutions like Operation Safe
Road fell on deaf ears.

There was something deeper at work. Like a can-
cer that had grown resistant to the usual courses
of treatment, Illinois corruption morphed, survived
and grew. The Governor's office changed personnel
and party affiliation, but the corruption persisted.

II. The Real Cost of Corruption

Why should the average person care about Illinois' culture of corruption? The answer—based on what I saw time and again as a public corruption prosecutor—is pretty straightforward: Citizens should care because corruption costs us. We pay dearly for corruption, not only in "hard" financial costs but also in the very real human costs that are more difficult to quantify. Ultimately, when corruption continues unabated for decades, it is far too easy for us to throw up our hands and begin to opt out of the political process. When this happens, we collectively suffer a most severe consequence: loss of faith in democracy itself.

Even with the steady chorus of voices against corruption over the past decade in Illinois, too little attention has been given to the real, actual costs of our tolerance of it. In my travels as a federal prosecutor and as the chair of the Illinois Reform Commission (IRC), I often heard good and decent people talk about Illinois' political scandals—the indictments, convictions, and prison sentences—as if they were spectators at a sporting event watching an entertaining match unfold. Truth be told, we do seem to dwell on the perverse entertainment value that these scandals provide. One recent example comes quickly to mind. When former Governor Rod Blagojevich petitioned the court to go to Costa Rica to eat bugs in the jungle as part of a proposed reality show, the media dutifully reported the event with front-page headlines and a large camera scrum outside the federal building. While I understand the tabloid-type interest in that event (I certainly watched and read closely myself), at some point that focus does a disservice to the real underlying losses we are experiencing in our body politic.

Many of us at times express embarrassment at the political scandals, particularly when the scandals provide constant fodder for late night comedians or editorial page writers. Yet, even here, the expressions of embarrassment regarding a particular politician's actions are often followed with a sense of resignation: "This is Illinois; what do you expect?"

Citizens should care because corruption costs us.

In the wake of scandals, politicians can be relied upon to voice, often loudly, expressions of outrage. We saw much of that during the Blagojevich impeachment proceedings, from both sides of the aisle. However, these reactions are notoriously short-lived. In addition, there is a strain of thought from the political establishment that the cure to any given corruption scandal is simply to purge the bad actor or actors from the government. By this way of thinking, for example, once Blagojevich was impeached and unceremoniously pushed off the stage, our problems were resolved and we could go back to business as usual.

While these reactions to scandal—by the citizens, the media, and politicians—are understandable, they fundamentally miss the central point about corruption: In many respects, the key problem we face in reforming our state is a collective failure to appreciate how much the corruption costs each of us personally. While the exceptional cases—such as the Willis family's experience—occasionally bring some temporary perspective about the human costs, this happens quite rarely.

At its core, the culture of corruption in Illinois is built upon some fairly basic realities. Government officials, elected and appointed, have the power to award contracts, leases, jobs, and scholarships; make appointments; and hand out other official goodies. Those who want the government goodies have the resources to provide benefits to the government officials (whether in the form of campaign contributions, wining and dining, vacation junkets, private sector jobs for relatives, or other acts of "friendship") in order to position themselves to receive these governmental goodies. What typically takes a back seat in this equation—or gets lost altogether—is what is best for the constituents of the government official. And the more significant and valuable the government "goodie" at issue, the more the merits of the decision seem to get lost in the shuffle.

What are the costs of this type of pay-to-play corruption? First, we pay a steep "corruption tax"—the value of taxpayer-financed waste, fraud, and abuse. During our IRC hearings, we heard testimony that estimated the annual Illinois corruption tax at $500 million per year in hard dollars. A 2009 study by Professor Richard Simpson and his University of Illinois Department of Political Science team, which attempted to quantify the hard costs of corruption, reached a similar result. While these specific estimates are obviously subject to debate, no one can credibly argue that the "hard" costs are minimal.

> *The annual Illinois corruption tax is estimated at $500 million per year in hard dollars.*

These hard costs of corruption include:
1. Lucrative leases and contracts (demonstrated in the Ryan trial and alleged in the Blagojevich investigation) that are priced above-market and often awarded with no meaningful competitive process. In some cases, the contracts are wholly unnecessary or are make-work projects designed only to reward the insider with a government goodie.
2. Government grants and programs (such as those alleged in the Blagojevich investigation) that are awarded to campaign contributors or others who have "paid to play" with no serious consideration of the merits.
3. Important governmental policy decisions (such as

33

which hospitals should be allowed to expand as discussed in Chapter VII) that are made on the basis of whether or not applicants will "pay to play."

4. Highly valuable jobs and promotions (whether as a city building inspector or a position as a deputy Sheriff's officer) that are given fraudulently. In some cases, the positions are created as make-work or "ghost" jobs that provide no value-added to the taxpayer.

This list goes on and on. But it doesn't end there. What about other real, but difficult to quantify, costs of corruption:

1. How much do we pay when insiders hijack the governmental decision-making process to serve a private agenda? For example, in the last two gubernatorial administrations, individuals close to the governor *who had no official position whatsoever with the government* sat at the table—quite literally—when important government decisions were being made. These insiders ran, in some key respects, a shadow government that was not accountable to the normal checks and balances of government. They made personnel, contract, and

lease decisions and helped dictate the governmental policy agenda. Almost always, they did so with their own agendas foremost in mind.

Individuals close to the governor who had no official position whatsoever with the government sat at the table when important decisions were being made.

2. How much do we pay when high-quality vendors refuse to participate in Illinois projects and take their wares elsewhere? As we heard during our IRC hearings, due to Illinois' reputation and the sense that the process is rigged for the clouted, some high-quality vendors simply will not compete in Illinois.

3. How much do we pay in loss of confidence in our system when citizens conclude that their son or daughter may have lost a spot at our flagship college institution because a public official or insider with clout exerted improper influence to secure admission for an under-qualified student? How about when a legislative scholarship is awarded to the son or daughter of a large campaign contributor? It is often these types of scenarios that cause a gut-level reaction of outrage in citizens.

Why? Perhaps because it's easier for folks to see more directly how this corruption costs *them*.

These types of scenarios cause a gut-level reaction of outrage in citizens.

---

4. How much did it cost the Willis family and others who are tangible, human victims of the culture of corruption? No further discussion is necessary here. The cost is incalculable, and the grief unimaginable.

I'd like to make an important point about the Willis incident. I do not believe it is fair to blame the 1994 Guzman incident *itself* on George Ryan *personally*. Specifically, there is no evidence that Ryan knew, before the fact, that the license examiner that sold Guzman his license was corrupt. What I do think we proved is that Ryan facilitated the culture of corruption in his office by the specific actions he and his office took regarding his internal investigators and the post-incident sweeping under the carpet. What Ryan's inspector general and several top officials knew, and what Ryan knew or should have known, is that the licenses-for-bribes mentality was a very direct outgrowth of the corrupt system they fostered and developed. Furthermore, when questions began to surface about the illicit connection between the licensing process and raising campaign funds, Ryan and his top people took affirmative actions to shut down the investigative activity. In March of 2000, then-Governor Ryan was asked about the corruption that occurred on his watch as Secretary of State. Ryan said matter-of-factly, "It was there when I was there, probably going to be there in the future. It's part of the culture there, I guess." Not exactly the comments of a leader who understood the costs we incur for corruption and pushed back against it.

That leads me to my final point here. When I refer to the "culture of corruption," I do not use the term in a way that would absolve public officials of personal responsibility and accountability. To the contrary, the circle of responsibility should extend to all who participate and advance that culture, as well as those who do nothing to thwart it. Further, at some point, even we citizens bear responsibility for failing to reform the culture when we see the problems and do nothing about them.

III. A Call from a Future Governor

On December 29, 2008, almost two years after I had left the prosecutor's office and a few short weeks after our corruption-fatigued state was jolted with the salacious public corruption allegations involving Governor Rod Blagojevich, I received an unexpected call from then Lt. Governor Pat Quinn.

Noting the disturbing events surrounding the recent arrest of Blagojevich, Quinn told me that we had an "integrity crisis" in Illinois. Citing my background as a former public corruption prosecutor, Quinn asked if I would be willing to serve as chairman of a volunteer reform commission to propose necessary and urgent reforms, including reforms requiring legislative action, for our state government.

I was simultaneously honored and skeptical—honored to receive a call to serve in this volunteer capacity but, having seen firsthand the underbelly of our political process for over a decade as a federal prosecutor, skeptical that the latest political scandal would spur the political system to meaningful action. If the Blagojevich Administration hadn't taken to heart the strong message that was sent via the prosecution of his predecessor George Ryan, how receptive would the state legislature be to the notion that we had a "culture of corruption" problem, not merely a Blagojevich problem? Yet, something about the Blagojevich allegations—and the attendant national publicity—made me think maybe, just maybe, these events could be the catalyst to cause public officials and everyday Illinois citizens to embrace a meaningful reform message.

Just maybe these events could be the catalyst to cause public officials and everyday Illinois citizens to embrace a meaningful reform message.

I agreed to meet with Quinn to discuss his vision for this endeavor. At our meeting, we discussed the concept of a citizen's commission—something like a jury—where citizens from diverse backgrounds and life experiences would rally around a common reform objective. During my conversations with Quinn, I asked for two things: the authority to help pick the members of this citizen's jury and, at the end of our independent work, authority to release our report to the public and "let the chips fall where they may." The soon-to-be governor readily agreed and honored the requests.

When I came back from the meeting and began reflecting on who might be good members of this citizen's jury, I knew immediately whom I would call first: Scott Willis. Over our eight-year investigation, the entire prosecutive team had come to know and greatly admire Scott and his wife, Janet. Years before Ryan's trial actually took place, their experience with the culture of corruption had become a motivating force for our work.

In early 2009, when I called Scott, he and Janet were living peacefully in a quiet little town in Tennessee. When I asked Scott if he would serve on the new commission, I considered it a long shot. Why would he do it? His family had been devastated by corruption. He owed nothing to Illinois, its political system, or me. Yet, much to my surprise, after taking some time for reflection and prayer, he answered the call and agreed to serve. While he quickly became the conscience of our commission, he was also a very active member who brought with him the common sense of the heartland.

Thirteen others—from all walks of life and with varying degrees of interactions with and impressions of state government—also answered the call to serve. We were educators, law enforcement personnel, military veterans, current and former public officials, not-for-profit organization heads, business leaders, an award-winning journalist, a corruption whistleblower, and even a college football coach. In mid-January, shortly after Lt. Governor Quinn became Governor Quinn, he issued his first Executive Order, creating and empowering this fifteen-person citizen's "jury," known as the Illinois Reform Commission (IRC).

Within days of the IRC's formation, we received a not-so-subtle message about the type of reception that awaited us in Springfield. Unbeknownst to me, one of our commission members received an unexpected call from a top aide to Speaker Michael Madigan. He asked the member to meet for coffee to discuss "ideas on ethics reform," and the member agreed to meet. However, instead of any discussion or exchange of substantive ideas on ethics reform, the aide essentially proposed that the IRC cut a deal with the legislature up front in order to avoid, as the aide put it, a direct "confrontation" with the legislative leadership. When I received word of this visit, I passed on the information of the not-so-subtle message we were being sent to my fellow commissioners. Our decision: There would be no backroom deals; we would roll up our sleeves, get to work, and generate a thoughtful product for the public.

Our decision: There would be no backroom deals; we would roll up our sleeves, get to work, and generate a thoughtful product for the public.

And that we did. In 100 days, we traveled to Rockford in the north, Carbondale in the south, and many points in-between to listen to citizens' views about their state government. We created and maintained a website, held town hall meetings, reviewed reams of information on our chosen topics, studied reforms implemented by other states, and conducted substantive hearings on six core topics. Then, after thousands of hours of meetings, conference calls, document review, report drafting, and the publishing of an interim report, the IRC and our volunteer staff released to Governor Quinn and the public our full 100-Day Report, in which we detailed our unanimous blueprint for reform. (To review the full IRC report, please go to www.reformillinoisnow.org).

Writing that report, as it turned out, was the easy part. While our 100-Day Report generally received favorable reviews from the general public and the media, many of our core proposals met stiff opposition in Springfield. We were told that we were asking for too much too soon, and that we did not appreciate the incremental nature of the democratic process. Others in Springfield sent a more blunt message: Most of our ideas were DOA (dead on arrival). With regard to some of our proposals focused on reforming the legislative process itself, the general response was: Legislators aren't the ones being indicted, so why are these legislature-directed reforms even being proposed? Our legislative critics knew we had a difficult, if not impossible, task if we were to succeed as outsiders in an insider's game. In the short term, they were right. Admittedly, we did not adopt a particularly sophisticated legislative strategy, nor did we adeptly compete in the Springfield "behind closed doors" way of doing business.

Collectively, we had few illusions that the proponents of the status quo would somehow overnight embrace our proposals. We had been selected at the beginning of a legislative session and time was against us. Nonetheless, as we were attempting to seize on this unique moment in our state's history, we viewed our principal job as proposing fundamental, battle-tested solutions to the process. We wanted to set a high, but achievable, bar for reform.

Ultimately, at the end of the IRC's tenure, only discrete portions of some of the reform proposals that we and other reform groups advanced were adopted. Most were not, and the reason is simple. With none of the major Democratic powerbrokers willing to champion our cause or seriously consider our proposed legislation, the most significant proposals were rejected or simply ignored.

Major reforms that struck at the heart of the culture of corruption—at least as we defined it—would have to wait until another day. Blagojevich and Ryan were indeed ousted and some partial victories won, but only the strongest proponents of the status quo would declare that the reform movement had won in 2009.

To most of us, the effort for meaningful reform had missed a unique opportunity to change the game. Instead, the journey had just begun.

IV. A Call to Action

In reflecting on my recent experiences as IRC chair, as well as my prior decade of service as a public corruption prosecutor, it would be far too easy to discourage citizens from engaging in the push for political reform in Illinois; rather, it would be far simpler for us to simply curse the darkness that is part of the Illinois political process.

Yet, we can't choose that easy route. Too much is at stake for all of us. Rather, people of good faith in Illinois have to engage—or re-engage—with our state government in collective, organized, and smart ways. And while we must be willing to compromise, we must also start winning. We must seek and obtain tangible reforms and not settle for symbolic gestures that will not change the game in Springfield—

and across the state—as it has been played for too many years.

So what do we do to reverse these debilitating trends?

First, we all need to understand that it won't be easy, nor will it happen overnight. It will take a concerted, long-term effort by participants in our democracy who will make a conscious choice and a long-term commitment to help restore a vibrant democracy in our state.

Second, reform in Illinois can no longer be a spectator sport, or the punch line to a joke. Rather, the reform effort needs to become an organized movement in which meaningful contributions are made from participants across the political spectrum.

Reform in Illinois can no longer be a spectator sport, or the punch line to a joke.

Third, we need a smart reform agenda. It should be an agenda that sets a high, but achievable, bar for reform. Most of the rest of this book will be devoted to discussing some of my thoughts on meaningful, game-changing reforms. Specifically, and borrowing heavily from the IRC experience, I propose a four-pronged reform agenda—addressing both the cul-

ture of corruption and our dysfunctional democracy:
1. Passing true campaign finance reform,
2. Creating a fair and competitive election process,
3. Enhancing corruption-fighting tools, and
4. Improving voter access and participation,

Fourth, we need three critical components, functioning in unison, to advance the reform agenda:
1. An informed, engaged, and organized citizenry,
2. Civic-minded, non-partisan institutional players, and
3. Independent-minded public servants, including elected officials, government employees, and new volunteers on Illinois state boards and commissions.

With any reform effort there must be a sense of passion and urgency—two qualities that were generally lacking in the legislative consideration of our IRC proposals and other reform efforts. While the effort to re-capture our government should begin in earnest during this 2010 election cycle, it cannot end there. All of us who join in this rebuilding process must make a new commitment to civic engagement—not just during a particular election but 24/7, 365 days a year. A tall order? Yes, but a necessary one in order to undo years of our allowing a culture of corruption to take hold in our state.

One ironic benefit of our scandal-plagued recent past is that neither of our two principal political parties owns the reform agenda, but either—or both—can be redeemed by it. Further, our democracy will benefit from a healthy competition among the two main political parties and committed independents to carry the banner for meaningful reform. This agenda is not a partisan one and can be embraced by activists on the right and on the left. Most critically, however, this agenda can also energize the millions who reside between the two ideological extremes to demand new and better government in Illinois.

With any reform effort, there must be a sense of passion and urgency.

Such an effort will require significant work, compromise, respect for others, open-mindedness, endurance, and creativity.

My experiences as a federal prosecutor and as the IRC chair also have led me to conclude that without a meaningful reform movement we will continue to reform by indictment and lawsuit. We have been there and done that, and it simply does not work. It is disappointing that the prosecution of former Governor Ryan did nothing to deter the alleged misconduct of his successor, former Governor Blagojevich, and his cohorts. There is a lesson here. The courts and prosecutors cannot be the sole path to game-changing reform; litigation often moves at a glacially slow pace, is narrowly focused, and always looks backward instead of forward. There is something deeper at work here in Illinois that prosecutions and civil lawsuits alone cannot mend.

Such an effort will require significant work, compromise, respect for others, open-mindedness, endurance, and creativity.

At the end of the day, in a democracy, we citizens will get the reform we *earn*. The real question is whether or not we are willing to move the democratic system passionately, collectively, and continuously to demand meaningful reform. If we are, then over time we can return the State of Illinois to its rightful place as a model of integrity for our entire nation.

By advancing these proposals, I do not seek to demonize all elected officials and the many men and women who serve in government across Illinois. I myself proudly served in government for twelve years, and in my governmental travels, including my recent experience as IRC chair, I have come across many honest and hard-working employees of city, county, state, and federal government, as well as dedicated and thoughtful elected officials in Springfield. Key Republicans and a handful of rank-and-file Democrats were supportive of our cause. Government service can and should be a noble calling, and we need to provide support to those in government who very much want to do the right thing.

In many respects, I think our job as citizens is to inspire our public officials and government employees across the state to take positive steps that, over time, will change the political culture in Illinois. On this topic, it is the citizens who must lead.

V. Campaign Finance Reform: Finishing What Was Started

It has been said that money is the mother's milk of politics. Candidates need to raise money to be competitive and ultimately win. Further, giving money to a favorite candidate is constitutionally-protected speech and is an important way for citizens to express their support of a candidate's views and ideas. However, during my years as a prosecutor, I also saw the dark side of campaign finance. In my investigations, campaign contributions were, almost always, the grease that kept the corruption machine churning. How so?

Over the years of my investigating public corruption, virtually every major investigation had a campaign finance problem. In Operation Safe Road, it started with the selling of licenses for bribes that were then funneled to George Ryan's campaign fund and graduated to the steering of leases, contracts, and even low-digit vanity license plates to large campaign contributors. In a number of other investigations, including the City of Chicago's Hired Truck investigation and the Sheriff's office case, department officials traded jobs and contracts for campaign contributions to favored politicians. Most recently, the allegations that former Governor Blagojevich considered trading the Obama Senate seat for campaign contributions or other benefits took pay-to-play politics in Illinois to a new low.

As I noted earlier, government officials have the power to award contracts, leases, jobs, scholarships, and other official goodies. Those who want the government goodies often give campaign funds to position themselves to receive these goodies. It is important to note that the First Amendment right to make campaign contributions of one's choosing only gives way when there is a "quid pro quo"—an agreement that a government official will make an official act in return for the campaign contribution.

Anything short of an explicit deal will be difficult to challenge. Not surprisingly, then, the more powerful and sophisticated politicians, who have more goodies to dispense, often amass the largest campaign war chests. Further, politicians and those individuals and organizations that might want the goodies have become quite adept at playing the game in a way that doesn't violate the "quid pro quo" threshold. This is, and will continue to be, a fact of political life.

> *The more powerful and sophisticated politicians, who have more goodies to dispense, often amass the largest campaign war chests.*

Can one law or series of campaign finance laws eradicate pay-to-play politics by themselves? Not a chance. It is true that some money will find its way into the system. It's also true that, given the fact that contributions start with bedrock constitutional protection, any limitation system has to be well thought out.

But does that mean we should do nothing? Until very recently, Illinois' answer apparently was yes. Adopting a "Wild, Wild West" theme, Illinois chose to sit idly by as we experienced never-before-seen expenditures in judicial elections, out-of-control spending on legislative and statewide races, and campaign finance scandals that have brought down the last two governors and dozens of other public officials.

As part of the Illinois Reform Commission's (IRC's) deliberative process, we routinely looked outside of Illinois for battle-tested efforts to improve democracy. In the "laboratories of democracy" among the 49 other states, there really is much to consider.

As we looked around the nation at the various approaches to campaign finance, we saw that Illinois came up far short. Even though our system was broken, for years we remained one of a handful of states that did not regulate or limit campaign contributions in any way. That's right, until an initial 2008 pay-to-play law (that was limited and had significant flaws), we had no laws restricting or controlling campaign contributions.

Along the way, this lack of action allowed a growing cynicism to creep in—one that caused average citizens in Illinois to assume that most things in government were for sale to the highest bidder.

---

*This lack of action allowed
a growing cynicism to creep in.*

The most serious effort to bring Illinois into the mainstream of campaign finance restrictions occurred last year. In 2009, the IRC, backed by other reform groups, proposed that Illinois take several significant steps in the campaign finance arena. Specifically, our three core proposals were:

1. To impose across-the-board limits on contributions to political campaigns similar to those enacted by the federal system. The limits were rooted in a basic premise: Why should someone be able to give more to a candidate for state representative than to a candidate for President of the United States?

2. To enact a pilot project for public financing of judicial elections in 2010, with an eye toward expanding the program if successful. The initial program would be narrowly targeted to prevent pay-to-play corruption in an area of government where neutrality is paramount: the judiciary.

3. To require real-time disclosure of significant contributions in order to give the public access to key and timely information about where officials were receiving financial support.

As to the contributions limits, a cursory review of the fundraising habits of the last three elected governors in Illinois shows the explosive growth in the influence of big money contributions. In eight years in office, former Governor Jim Edgar raised $11.8 million, with only eight contributions exceeding $25,000. In four years in office, former Governor George Ryan raised $20 million, with "only" thirty-five contributions over $25,000. Most recently, in his six years in office, former Governor Rod Blagojevich raised $58 million, including a whopping *435 contributions over $25,000*. And therein lies the principal problem that contribution limits address head-on. When someone is giving $25,000, unless it's a very close relative or long-time friend, he or she probably wants something specific from government. And while, as a prosecutor, I saw public officials sell their office for the mere sums of $500 and $1,000, the fact is that corrupt public officeholders rarely come that cheap. On the flipside, contributions of $25,000 almost always come with serious strings attached.

This is a "low-hanging fruit" problem that contribution limits attempt to address. That is, we can do a lot just by limiting the amount any one person or organization can give to a particular candidate. The IRC believed it appropriate to start—but not end—there.

I will discuss later the wholly unsatisfactory democratic "process" we encountered in attempting to advance campaign finance reform in 2009. However, for now, a word or two is in order here about the substance of the ultimate campaign finance bill that the legislature passed last fall and Governor Quinn signed. The campaign finance bills—both the one that was sponsored by the Democratic leadership that initially passed in the spring over the IRC's objection, as well as the revised bill that passed in the fall session—adopted the contribution limits concept, but with an important, and I would argue fatal, provision. The fundamental flaw in both bills was the failure to restrict the contributions legislative leaders from either party can give to candidates for office.

The fundamental flaw was the failure to restrict the contributions legislative leaders can give.

Why is that a major problem? There are two main reasons. First, the legislative leaders, particularly those of the party in power, wield enormous influence over the legislative process as is. To give each of them, in effect, an additional significant point of leverage by allowing them—and only them—an unlimited ability to financially support (or punish) the candidates of their choice only seeks to increase their already formidable power. Second, when this power to give unlimited funds is a benefit they *alone* have—when the rest of us are substantially limited in how much we can give to any one candidate—it only serves to increase their relative power.

Let me give a quick example. Say there is a race between a challenger and a leadership-supported incumbent. Under existing law, an individual or organization could give large amounts—$100,000 or more—to the challenger to try to help that candidate be competitive with the leadership-sponsored candidate who also could receive unlimited funds—$100,000 or more—from leadership. With the new limits imposed, the challenger can only receive $5,000 (from an individual) or $10,000 (from an organization). Yet, under the same new rules, the legislative leader's committee can continue to give *unlimited* amounts in general elections. The existing power and unlimited funding ability is a double whammy that will make challenges to incumbents even more difficult than they already are. And we need more, rather than fewer, challenges to incumbents. We should press hard to fix this law and limit contributions across the board.

While future events will show whether the gaping loophole in the new campaign finance law will be remedied, in the long-run there is perhaps an even bigger disappointment from the 2009 legislative session. Specifically, the legislature missed a golden opportunity to adopt a public finance pilot project as the IRC proposed. Actually, our proposal was not a novel concept—almost half the states have tried public finance in one form or another. Further, prior to 2009, Illinois legislators had considered several bills that proposed the very form of public finance pilot project that the IRC proposed.

The idea was to conduct a serious test of public finance by focusing on judicial races, where virtually everyone can agree that campaign contributions (particularly those made by lawyers) could distort the justice system. Under the current rules in place until 2011, any lawyer can give any amount (even $100,000 or more) to a judicial candidate and, conceivably, present his or her case before the judge shortly thereafter. Even with contribution limits recently enacted, an individual lawyer could give a judge hearing the lawyer's case $5,000 every year, and his or her law firm could give another $10,000 as well. That is unseemly, at best.

What is public finance and why should we give it a

try? In a nutshell, public finance provides a mechanism for candidates who demonstrate certain levels of basic support to access a public pool of money to finance their campaigns. This allows the candidate to avoid groveling for money (or worse) from vested interests and focus on the strength of his or her message. While there are various versions of public finance, at the most basic level, candidates who opt-in to the public finance system must go out and obtain a certain amount of small contributions to show their viability (sort of like getting a certain number of signatures on nominating petitions). Once that established threshold is met (say 500 contributors of $50 each), the candidate qualifies for a stipend from the state in return for agreeing to limit overall spending for the campaign.

> *Public finance provides a mechanism for candidates who demonstrate certain levels of basic support to access a public pool of money to finance their campaigns.*

While the overall results have been mixed in states that have tried public finance, there are two important documented benefits to a well-run public finance system. First, the number of grassroots contributors to campaigns grows. More people give smaller amounts because their donation, even when small, will matter. Second, the diversity of candidates grows as candidates no longer have to rely on the "old-boy network" to raise their funds. Yes, there is a financial cost to taxpayers of a public finance system, and that certainly makes adopting such a system less attractive, especially in difficult economic times.

Yet that shouldn't deter us from taking a hard look for two reasons. First, any public funds utilized for a pilot project would pale in comparison to the portion of the "corruption tax" we all pay because of pay-to-play politics. Second, funding for public financing can be tied specifically to the users of the specific system for which the elections are being held. For example, as the IRC proposed for judicial campaigns, we might look at raising funds by increasing judicial fines or penalties. Better yet, maybe we can increase the license fees lawyers pay. Who could be against taxing the lawyers? There are other options to fund a pilot project to avoid a general tax increase, and we should look at them.

So what happened to the legislature's consideration of a pilot public finance project? Well, instead of dusting off one of the bills that had been kicking around the legislature for several years that sought a judicial public finance program, the legislature, as part of their 2009 "reform," settled for a three-year study of the issue due to be completed in 2012. There is no good reason we need to go backwards and simply commit to more and more study. Public financing of elections has been studied to death. Better yet, it has been implemented in one form or another in 25 other states. It's time to try it on a small but important scale and see if we can do it right and whether or not it works.

> *There is no good reason we need to go backwards and simply commit to more and more study.*

There is another aspect of campaign finance reform that needs more discussion, and this relates to the "expenditure" side of campaigns—how candidates spend the money they raise. The fact of the matter is that, particularly for high-profile races, most of a campaign's budget is dedicated to "voter contact"—getting the candidate known and getting its message out to the public. And in Illinois—for statewide races at least—that means using television. It is more than a bit ironic that candidates spend so much time raising money from the public, only to spend it on the use of television ads over public airways. While we only touched on this briefly in our IRC work, a related form of public funding that should be considered is the use of free airtime for the candidates to get their messages across. If candidates were allowed access to the airwaves in some fair manner, wouldn't this help put a dent in the insatiable appetite candidates have for campaign dollars? Isn't it likely that campaigns would then be more focused on the merits of the policies and unique characteristics of the candidates and less about their ability to get substantial contributions from people, including people who have vested interests in government? This is something that merits more study and should be pursued.

As to the third prong of the IRC's campaign finance reform—year-round "real time" reporting—the legislature acknowledged that, under the current system, there is too large a window (as long as seven months in some instances) between the receipt of a contribution and the time it has to be reported to the public. A simple example illustrates the problem. In March, during the midst of the spring legislative session, a contributor currently can give an elected official a large contribution, and yet the public would not learn of the contribution until the campaign files its semi-annual reports in July. By that time, the legislative session would be over with votes taken and legislation passed. Yet the contributor's self-interest would not yet have been disclosed to the public. While the campaign finance reform passed in the fall of 2009 began to address the disclosure issue, it did not go as far as the IRC proposed. And for those who think any attempt to actually limit contributions is foolhardy, this real-time disclosure provision takes on added significance. At the very least, it provides the public with information we do not currently have and gives investigative reporters and a candidate's opponent a chance to tell us about troubling contributions *before* the election and vote.

VI. Should We Pick Our Leaders or Should They Pick Us?

In our representative democracy, it is a fundamental right for the voters to pick their representatives. When we go to the polls, we have the right to elect our legislative representatives, both in Springfield and Washington D.C., to represent our particular geographic region's interests. The specific legislative candidates who are offered to us are determined in large part by a "redistricting" process that occurs every ten years, after the completion of the national census. That process results in our state being divided up into a number of legislative districts, for both state and federal offices, with approximately the same number of voters in each district.

However, in Illinois, we have a redistricting process that turns this fundamental right of voters on its head. For years, the leaders of both political parties have capitalized on a winner-take-all "redistricting" process whereby one political party draws legislative districts—for both state and federal offices—behind closed doors to protect favored incumbents.

In Illinois, we have a redistricting process that turns this fundamental right of voters on its head.

This system of redistricting is the cornerstone of the "Incumbent Protection Act," a sarcastic reference to the series of self-serving provisions our government has embraced that exclude challengers and prevent voters from advancing meaningful change to our system. As such, Illinois' redistricting process must be challenged in a coordinated manner by us citizens. Simply put, the current redistricting system has distorted our democracy and must be changed. The good news is that the redistricting process *can be* changed directly by the voters, without the need to have Springfield insiders who are responsible for

68

the current system lead the effort. The bad news is that a lot of coordinated effort and hard work is necessary to change the game, and it must be done *now*.

I must admit that it took some time for me to come around to the conclusion that redistricting was a critical, game-changing issue. When I entered into the IRC process, I came to the table believing that an overhaul of our campaign finance system was the cornerstone of ethical reform in Illinois. While I still believe that meaningful campaign finance reform is a key to the reform agenda, redistricting should be discussed at the same time and with equal immediacy. After talking to redistricting experts (brought to us by IRC point person Brad McMillan), hearing citizens speak at our town hall meetings, studying other states' experiences, and living through a disheartening Springfield legislative experience, I have moved redistricting reform to the top of the reform agenda. It also has the important advantage of being something we citizens can advance *now*.

While redistricting may not be as sexy as campaign finance reform or draw the headlines that campaign finance scandals have produced, our current process of redrawing our election districts exposes an even more fundamental flaw in Illinois democracy. Our current system of redistricting has severed a fundamental, essential connection that voters have to their elected officials: responsiveness to their constituents. That is, elected leaders who are created by a severely flawed redistricting process need not listen closely to their constituents because essentially *they* have picked *their* constituents, rather than the *voters* having picked *their* leaders. The result is a set of incumbents who are effectively insulated from the electoral process.

Elected leaders have picked their constituents, rather than the voters having picked their leaders.

How does the current redistricting process work in Illinois? I will admit that, before the IRC process, I didn't have a clue. Unless you are a very well informed citizen or student of government, you would be surprised and dismayed about how we go about this important process in Illinois. Every ten years, after we receive the results of the national census, the political operatives get together in a series of closed-door sessions and carve up Illinois like a Thanksgiving turkey. According to the Illinois State Constitution, the resulting districts are to be "compact and contiguous," that is, as small and connected as possible and without gaps. While the lack of transparency in this process is a time-honored tradition in Springfield, the lack of public review of the map-drawing process has increased the use of anti-democratic criteria to draw the important electoral boundaries in our state. With no meaningful public input or scrutiny of the internal process, the politicians do what politicians do: They reward their friends, punish their enemies, cut deals, and work to prolong their own tenure in office.

With no meaningful public input or scrutiny of the internal process, the politicians do what politicians do.

The notorious "tie-breaking" provision of the current process in Illinois is perhaps the most ludicrous of all. When the current process called for in the Illinois State Constitution does not result in an agreed-upon map by a majority of the legislature (which it rarely does), then the Illinois Constitution provides that a lottery be conducted to, in effect, choose which party will be able to control the process. (In fairness to the framers of our present Constitution, this provision was meant to be so unpalatable that no legislature would ever fail to reach a majority and thus resort to using such a risky provision.) Yet, in Illinois, after three of the last four censuses, this "lottery" provision has been triggered. Twice, the Democrats won the coin toss and got to redistrict the state to their specifications; and the other time, the Republicans won. In all three cases, the citizens lost.

In all three cases, the citizens lost.

The actual lottery process is dripping with ironic symbolism. When a map cannot be agreed upon by the legislature, a "ceremony" is held in a room in the Old State Capitol in Springfield. At the ceremony, officials bring into the room a replica of President Abraham Lincoln's stovepipe hat. Placed inside the hat are two names. One is for the Republicans and the other for the Democrats. Illinois' Secretary of State then reaches into Honest Abe's hat and selects one party as the winner. And that is how we decide which party gets control of the redistricting process in Illinois for the next ten years. Whichever party wins, they no longer have to direct an even-handed process. They effectively get to draw the electoral districts in Illinois to serve their own partisan self-interest.

Our highest court in Illinois has criticized this lottery option, stating that "the rights of the voters should not be part of a game of chance." But our legislature has not heeded this criticism and has instead retained the status quo.

What is the result of redistricting, Illinois style? Illinois voters get a winner-take-all map that is biased and counterproductive to the democratic process. The result of this closed-door process is as remarkable as it is predictable: oddly-shaped legislative districts that are immune from serious electoral challenge and therefore protect powerful incumbent members of both parties (because, in order to make sure one party has "safe" districts, the party drawing the map will give a certain number of "safe" districts to the other party).

For example, following the last map process in 2002, 98% of the legislative elections have been won by the incumbents. Is that because the voters are almost unanimously satisfied with the legislative results that have been achieved? Hardly. It is because the election results are often guaranteed before the very first vote is cast. And the victims of this gerrymandered process? In addition to voters across Illinois, the losers of the process also include the relatively few independent-thinking legislators for whom the party bosses have little use. Without clout or loyalty chips to cash in, these legislators find themselves on the losing end of incumbency-protect-ing redistricting deals. Democracy suffers and the effects are compounded across the decades, as we build a legislature essentially immune from the electoral process. As a result, it grows more distant from the people.

What about the "compact and contiguous" requirement in the State Constitution? It is said that a picture tells a thousand words. For redistricting abuses, that picture is the Illinois 17th Congressional district *(pictured on the next page).*

One of the poster children for redistricting reform at the federal level, this gerrymandered district snakes from Illinois' western border at the Quad Cities, along the Mississippi River short of St. Louis, then across to Springfield and on further east to Decatur. Ignoring both the letter and the spirit of the state constitution, the 17th district is sprawling and amoeba-like. It pays no respect to municipal boundaries, geographic boundaries, or common regional issues. It and other districts like it were the result of political dealmaking that ignored the interests of the voters and ultimately our most deeply held democratic ideals.

A similar point can be made about the drawing of our state legislative districts. During the last redistricting effort engineered by the Democrats who won the lottery, the state Senate District 51

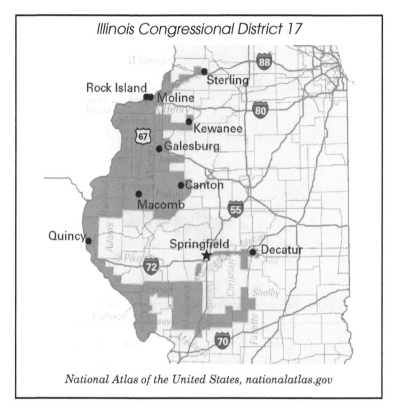

Illinois Congressional District 17

National Atlas of the United States, nationalatlas.gov

(pictured on the next page) was reconfigured to pit a number of incumbent Republicans against one another, including IRC member Duane Noland. The resulting shape defies geometric definition. It is 110 miles long from one end of the district to the other, and a comparatively narrow eight miles wide

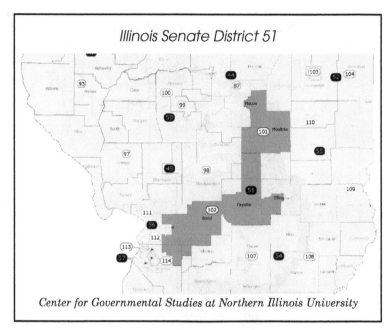

Illinois Senate District 51

Center for Governmental Studies at Northern Illinois University

in parts. A quick look at the contours of Senate 51 shows that the Democrats who drew the map were not thinking about the state's constitutionally-required "compact and contiguous" characteristics. Notably, after the new map was drawn, Senator Noland chose to retire, and the Senate lost an honorable member. A simple look at the state map reveals that geometric gamesmanship abounds. To be clear: When the Republicans won the lottery, they attempted to do the exact same thing to the Democrats.

One of the most memorable comments I heard at the IRC town hall meetings occurred in Rock Island, Illinois. On that evening, we were listening to voters talk about a host of issues that concerned them. A gentleman stood up, indicated he was retired, and commenting on the oddly shaped districts that are the hallmark of a gerrymandered legislative map, he said: "I'm an engineer by training. Why is it that Illinois doesn't know how to draw rectangles?" Perhaps not coincidentally, we were holding this town hall near the Illinois-Iowa border. Unlike us, our western neighbor, Iowa, has turned over the district-drawing process to a non-partisan computer and, not surprisingly, Iowa's districts resemble the familiar rectangular shape that our engineer would recognize.

Of course, Illinois is not Iowa, and our rich diversity is something that we must celebrate and account for in any reformed redistricting process. Indeed, the IRC proposal seeks to maximize minority representation and comply fully with federal law. So, while we probably cannot turn out perfect rectangles in Illinois, we can do a whole lot better than we have done. An improved system of redistricting will not simply yield a more geometrically friendly vision, but it will also fundamentally alter the responsiveness of the officials we elect.

Indeed, that was one of the key lessons of the IRC review of redistricting in other states. No state has a lottery process for redistricting like Illinois has, and many others have taken steps to de-politicize the process. In proposing meaningful redistricting reform, the IRC looked beyond our borders for a better way to do things. When we began discussions with legislative leaders about redistricting reform, however, we were told the process could be revisited later—after the legislature had an opportunity to propose a better solution. We are still waiting.

*No state has a lottery process
for redistricting like Illinois has.*

We should not and need not wait any longer. Redistricting reform, which would require a constitutional amendment, can be led by citizens, and it can happen now. If we work together, we can dramatically change the landscape on this crucial issue. As many folks know, we are currently in the midst of our national census. When the results of the 2010 census are completed, the redistricting process will begin again. The legislative map that is drawn will shape our politics and, in key respects, the quality of our democracy for the next ten years.

What specifically can we do? This year we have the opportunity to put on the November ballot a road-map for redistricting change. Officially dubbed the "Fair Map Amendment" and patterned after the IRC proposal, a meaningful redistricting reform effort is up and running. The beauty of this goal is that we, the people, can make this change, and the folks who live by the "Incumbent Protection Act" and benefit from the current system cannot stop us. However, to get a new redistricting process on the ballot as a constitutional amendment for the voters to consider, we need almost 300,000 valid signatures of Illinois voters by May 2010. A number of well-known Illinois reform groups who have fought valiantly for previous reforms are leading the Fair Map Amendment effort. You can log on to www.ilfairmap.com today, download a petition sheet, and obtain signatures to help the effort meet the signature requirement, and ultimately make redistricting reform a reality.

So what are the new, game-changing features of the Fair Map Amendment? While any formalized redistricting process will be necessarily complex, the Fair Map Amendment makes four key proposed changes to the current system:

1. Rather than legislative leaders drawing the map

to protect their respective turf, a nine-person, independent committee will propose the maps.

2. Rather than a map being drawn behind closed doors, the map-drawing process will be open and transparent.
3. Rather than permitting improper and overtly political factors to be considered in drawing a map, the map will be governed by specified criteria, including full compliance with the federal Voting Rights Act to ensure maximum minority participation.
4. Rather than conducting a lottery and providing a windfall to the winning political party, justices of the Illinois Supreme Court will pick an independent special master to draw a final map if agreement cannot be reached by the independent committee.

Of course, legislators do not need to wait until the Fair Map Amendment gets on the November ballot to propose change to the redistricting process. Legislative leaders could acknowledge the flaws of the current process and change the redistricting game themselves. Furthermore, if there are aspects of the Fair Map Amendment that are impractical or could be improved upon, they are welcome to advance a competing proposal. As with any legislatively-generated reform proposal, however, we would have to closely examine whether their proposal meets the criteria for game-changing reform or is just another smoke screen. Further, if history is any guide, it is quite unrealistic to expect the legislature to adopt a new, fairer system that would jeopardize their job security in Springfield. We welcome the day when we can trust our legislators to act in the public interest, but we simply cannot wait for that day. The time for citizens to reform the redistricting process is now.

We welcome the day when we can trust our legislators to act in the public interest, but we simply cannot wait for that day.

The guiding principles for any well-designed redistricting proposal *are not* complex. For the Fair Map Amendment, these principles are making the process more:
1. Independent;
2. Transparent;
3. Competitive; and
4. Fair.

Those are pretty good democratic principles.

Given the state of affairs in Illinois, the opponents of the Fair Map Amendment—and no doubt there are many insiders who will be against it—really have the burden to defend the status quo. What are the principles that undergird the current system? How can we continue to support a system that results in gerrymandered election districts on both the state and federal level? How can we continue to allow one party or the other—based on picking a name out of Abe Lincoln's hat—to redraw the election districts of Illinois to its partisan specifications?

The time to change the redistricting game in Illinois is now. And we have the power to do it.

VII. Recorded Conversations: The Best Evidence and the Best Deterrent

In 2003, Pam Davis, the CEO of Edwards Hospital, located in Naperville, Illinois, was attempting to expand her hospital to meet the medical needs of the growing western suburbs. However, before initiating the expansion, she needed the approval of a prominent Illinois state board. Now, I do not pretend to know whether her proposal deserved to be approved on its merits. What I do know, however, is that neither Edwards Hospital nor any other hospital expansion candidate deserved what followed. And what followed was a harsh lesson in Illinois' culture of corruption.

What followed was a harsh lesson in Illinois' culture of corruption.

According to Davis, she was told that if she wanted her hospital expansion approved, she would have to play ball and pay up. Ultimately, she did what few corporate leaders have ever done. She brought the information to law enforcement, and in this case, to federal agents and the FBI. She detailed her experience and, most importantly for the FBI, agreed to secretly record future conversations with those who were telling her that she had to "pay to play." Due to the federal tools the FBI has at its disposal, the agents immediately went to work. For several weeks, under the supervision of the FBI, Davis agreed to record conversations with state decision makers about her application. (As the individuals she spoke to were unaware that these conversations were being recorded, they are called "one-party consent" recordings.)

After obtaining valuable information from these one-party consent recordings and from other sources, the United States Attorney's office then took it up a notch. Prosecutors applied to a federal judge to obtain a court-authorized wiretap of the ringleader's phone. (The government has to go to a judge because the federal law requires that, before the government obtains the extraordinary power to secretly record conversations of *both* parties, a judge has to review the facts and evidence and ensure that the government has a proper basis to move forward for a period of time not to exceed 30 days). Once the judge approved the wiretap, it became an invaluable evidence-gathering device for the government. Federal agents secretly recorded all the relevant phone conversations of one of the principal wrongdoers, Stuart Levine, who was a member of the prominent state board deciding the fate of the Edwards Hospital expansion application.

For the government, the ability to record these conversations and follow the crimes by listening to the participants describe the scheme among themselves accelerated the case. While the machine was recording, Levine talked for weeks about corrupt arrangements he was engaged in with many powerful players in Illinois. Indictments of prominent members of the Blagojevich Administration soon followed, and Operation Board Games was successfully launched. The public benefited from this unraveling of a serious corrupt scheme, including a corrupt process that had made Pam Davis and many others victims of their own government.

> *The ability to record these conversations and follow the crimes by listening to the participants describe the scheme among themselves was a game-changer.*

In large part because of the example Davis set for corporate victims of pay-to-play corruption, I asked her to serve on the Illinois Reform Commission (IRC). She willingly agreed. Prior to serving with Davis, I had never met her and was only generally familiar with her personal story from press accounts. As she told her story and as we evaluated the law enforcement tools to fight corruption, I began to ask myself: What if Davis had gone to a state (instead of federal) law enforcement official—such as a county state's attorney? (After all, many of the alleged crimes would qualify as crimes under *either* state or federal law). Would the same result—the revelation of hard core pay-to-play corruption— have occurred? Without Davis setting the process in motion by going to federal authorities and being willing to record her conversations, would the federal government have obtained the key indictments and convictions that occurred in Operation Board Games?

To answer these questions, we need to understand the key law enforcement tools that the federal government has at its disposal and the fact that those same tools have been denied to our state's attorneys across Illinois.

I reflect back on my experience in Operation Safe Road, which, as described earlier, was also fueled by similar "one-party consent" recordings that led to court-approved federal wiretaps. The Operation Safe Road wiretaps allowed us to learn so many important things about the licenses-for-bribes scandal, including what was motivating some of the key criminal acts. Without the ability to secretly record conversations in a timely manner and seek court-authorized wiretaps, would we have been able to learn, let alone demonstrate in court, the fundraising ticket motive for some of the licenses-for-bribes activity? Would the investigation have escalated to expose the wrongdoing of high-ranking members of the Ryan Administration? In my opinion, the answer to both questions is no.

Then, of course, there is the current case involving former Governor Blagojevich. When he was arrested on December 9, 2008, the public learned that the federal government had recorded weeks of conversations involving the then-governor and his top aides, again pursuant to federal court-authorized wiretaps. According to the criminal complaint, our former governor described—in blunt and often profane terms in recorded conversations—his corrupt motives for a number of important governmental decisions he faced. One particular example stood out. As governor, he had the exclusive right to appoint an individual to the United States Senate to replace the newly elected President Obama. In discussing his appointment authority with others, as allegedly recorded on a court-ordered wiretap, our governor described the opportunity as "[bleepin] golden"—something he wasn't going to give away without getting something of benefit in return. While a jury will determine the legal import of this statement and others like it, the recordings will give the jury reliable real-time evidence of the governor's motives, unvarnished and in his own words.

Recorded evidence also has another real benefit: It is reliable. This is important not just to the government but also to defendants like Blagojevich and to the justice system itself. For example, in some of the public statements they have made already, Blagojevich and his legal team have embraced the substance of the recorded conversations, most of which the public has not yet heard but Blagojevich's legal team has. His legal team has argued that the words on the tapes, when heard in their totality, will exonerate him. A jury ultimately will decide that important issue, but isn't it a good thing for the justice system that both sides are pointing to the same reliable recorded evidence in an important criminal case?

Back to the key reform issue regarding recorded evidence: The simple fact is that in each of these noted occasions of high-profile corruption investigations the crimes committed were violations of both state and federal law, so they could be pursued by state *or* federal officials. However, in each of these situations, only federal law enforcement had the necessary tools to expose the significant corruption that existed.

Here is the kicker that most citizens of Illinois do not know: In Illinois, our state law enforcement officials do not have the authority to pursue court-ordered wiretaps in corruption cases, nor do they have the ability to authorize individual recorded conversations, such as those that occurred with Pam Davis' "one-party consent." The federal government and the governments of most other states—46 to be exact—have the authority to do "one-party consent" recordings and/or obtain state court-ordered wiretaps in public corruption cases. Would that be a good thing for our corruption plagued-state? Due to the proven track record of corruption at the municipal, county, and state level here, the IRC concluded yes. We need this law-enforcement tool—albeit properly applied and administered—enacted in our state so that well-trained officials of the state can utilize it under appropriate circumstances.

So, the two most significant corruption investigations in Illinois in over a generation—Operation Safe Road (involving Republican George Ryan's Administration) and Operation Board Games (involving Democrat Rod Blagojevich's Administration)— were fueled by two powerful tools available *only* to federal law enforcement: one-party consensually recorded conversations (by cooperating witnesses like Pam Davis) and federally court-ordered wiretaps. In both situations, I would contend that the availability of these critical tools was a necessary component of the investigation's success.

During the IRC process, we reviewed the authority that other states have been given and let our legislature know that Illinois was in the distinct minority on this issue. We also presented, in very practical terms, how these tools have dramatically advanced federal public corruption investigations in Illinois. We also pointed out that Illinois has a wiretap statute that allows for state court-authorized secret recordings; however, the legislature effectively has limited this wiretap authority to crimes involving guns, drugs, and gangs.

Serious public corruption crimes—like bribery and extortion—do not provide the basis for a state prosecutor to seek a wiretap from a state judge. Think about that: State law enforcement officials can wiretap drug dealers and gang leaders in Illinois, but under no circumstances can they obtain wiretaps for corruption cases, even when there exists substantial evidence of large-scale bribery. Why should that be?

State law enforcement officials cannot obtain wiretaps for corruption cases, even when there exists substantial evidence of large-scale bribery.

Now I admit that I am biased on this issue due to my prior experiences. However, I also acknowledge and respect the very real concerns that have been raised about the potential for governmental abuse of this awesome power. When we proposed to the legislature the idea of a wiretap statute that covered not just gang and drug crimes but corruption crimes as well, that is where opposition began. We were told that such a statute could be abused by state's attorneys who are publicly-elected and thus might use the statute for improper political purposes. We were also told that the federal government is doing a good job in this area and, therefore, they don't need any help. We were also told that state law enforcement officials would use it in a discriminatory and partisan fashion.

While I personally agree that a healthy skepticism of government—whether at the federal, state or local level—is always in order, I believe that legitimate concerns about potential abuses can be addressed satisfactorily, particularly when we continue to allow wiretaps for other serious crimes.

First, any statute can be abused by an ambitious prosecutor, whether that prosecutor is a federal one appointed by the President or a state one elected by the public. Moreover, if the wiretap statute is inherently subject to abuse, why should we let state-elected prosecutors have this authority for cases involving gangs, drugs, and gun investigations, as they have for years? I do not hear any prominent voices in the Illinois state legislature suggesting repeal of the present state statutes.

In order to address legitimate concerns of potential abuse, we should mandate formalized training for state law enforcement entities desiring to utilize wiretap authority. Moreover, states attorneys' offices that are serious about pursuing public corruption will have to add personnel trained in electronic surveillance to lead their corruption units. That's precisely what Anita Alvarez, the Cook County State's Attorney and an IRC member, did when she beefed up her public corruption unit by hiring Jack Blakey, a former federal prosecutor, to lead it. By hiring someone experienced in electronic surveillance issues, Alvarez has positioned her office well for any amendment in the law that would allow the state to utilize any enhanced tools that are approved.

As to the second argument, which is that the feds are doing a good job on the corruption issue, I do agree that federal law enforcement officials are quite adept at bringing public corruption cases. Yet, what people often forget is that federal law enforcement, particularly in a post 9/11 world, has limited resources to pursue corruption cases. People would be amazed at how few federal officials—both prosecutors and agents—work public corruption cases in

Chicago on a regular basis. Further, while the feds are probably second to none in pursuing cases of high-profile corruption involving high-level officials like governors, there are a lot of corruption allegations that are presented to federal officials but do not get ample resources dedicated to them. Many of those cannot be staffed by the feds based on their limited resources, but state officials could and would pursue these allegations with the appropriate tools and resources. Other times, it is not clear that federal laws have been broken, while state laws clearly have been. Should those cases not be pursued if there is a viable, well-trained alternative on the local level?

In short, federal law enforcement officials cannot work with every Pam Davis who might have information about a corrupt public official. Why not give the Pam Davises of the world a choice of which law enforcement officer—federal or state—should take and evaluate her information?

With a change in the law, that same choice should also be available to law enforcement officials such as David Hoffman, IRC member and the former City of Chicago Inspector General. Such officials, who are charged with investigating corruption but cannot prosecute cases themselves, need to have multiple outlets to bring information. If the state was a viable option, inspector generals would have more options to ensure corruption allegations receive the appropriate attention, particularly if the feds cannot take the case because of lack of resources.

Federal law enforcement officials cannot work with every Pam Davis who might have information about a corrupt public official.

Finally, much of the opposition to expanded authority for state prosecutors is rooted in the assumption that state prosecutors are more likely to act politically, and therefore irresponsibly, with evidence than federal prosecutors. While I appreciate that the motivations of a prosecutor who is publicly-elected are more easily subject to attack or second-guessing, we have to keep in mind what type of evidence we are talking about obtaining: *the actual words of the individuals under investigation.* The tape recording machine doesn't lie. Recorded evidence is not evidence that can be fabricated easily, and that's worth considering as we evaluate the likelihood of partisan abuse. Ultimately, as in the case of former Governor Blagojevich, the defendant often embraces the information on the tape, as it is less subject to government pressure and manipulation than, say, a government witness who may recount a version of events in return for obtaining a reduced sentence.

A recent public corruption investigation involving a state prosecutor illustrates several key points about publicly elected prosecutors evaluating high-profile prosecutions when recorded evidence is available. In 2009, U.S. Senator Roland Burris, a Democrat, was being investigated by John Schmidt, the publicly elected Republican Sangamon County State's Attorney. The investigation related to whether Burris lied under oath when he testified publicly before a legislative panel regarding his appointment to the Obama Senate seat. (As it was a public proceeding, Burris' testimony before the legislature happened to be recorded, though not pursuant to any wiretap statute.) The recorded evidence provided no doubt as to what Burris actually said under oath, as well as what the precise wording of the questions was—both key issues in a perjury case. The fact that we had precise evidence was a good thing for Burris, the prosecutor, and the justice system. From the politics of it, we had a case where a Republican state's attorney was investigating one of the state's highest-profile Democratic officials. Under the theory that publicly elected prosecutors will act politically and therefore irresponsibly, it should have been a no-brainer for Schmidt to indict Burris, right? Well, what actually happened was that the Republican Schmidt did not indict the Democrat Burris. Schmidt reviewed the evidence, which included tape-recorded evidence, and concluded that he did not have enough evidence to indict.

Now, I don't know John Schmidt, nor do I know the particular matters he weighed in his final decision, but I conclude that he acted the way the vast majority of prosecutors would act in a politically-charged case with recorded conversations: that is, cautiously. In important ways, recorded conversations can keep prosecutors more honest and reduce the likelihood that a case is politically-motivated or trumped up.

I believe the fundamental question for us, the citizens of Illinois, is this: How serious do we consider public corruption crimes to be? In Illinois, given our tattered history, don't they deserve to be mentioned in the same breath as other serious crimes, like possession or sale of illegal guns and drugs? If so, then why not give our state law enforcement officials the same time-honored tools that the federal government and 46 other states have to conduct "one-party consent" recordings and court-ordered wiretaps for a serious corruption offense?

Yes, let's discuss the potential abuses and build in protections and training that will reduce the possibility that abuses will occur. Let's also define the serious corruption offenses that could trigger the statute so that we don't allow for use of this awesome power for ticky-tack offenses. However, let's not kid ourselves: Illinois is in the minority of states by *not* giving its law enforcement officials the tools they need to fight political corruption. If we did, the only folks that would need to be nervous about the actions of ambitious state prosecutors would be corrupt politicians in Illinois. They should be nervous. As citizens of Illinois, we should *want* them to be nervous.

VIII. Do We Want People to Participate... or Not?

In order to complete a reform agenda discussion, we must take stock of the citizens' participation in the electoral process. At the core of a healthy and functioning democracy is a government that encourages civic participation in the political process and, after the elections are over, offers transparency in its government operations. In the spring of 2009, aided by the efforts of the Illinois Reform Commission (IRC) and our quarterback on this issue, Hanke Gratteau, the Illinois legislature took some important initial steps to improve transparency in government by amending the state's Freedom of Information Act (FOIA), the flagship transparency statute. A good start, but only a start.

In this chapter, I'd like to discuss four tangible reforms that would improve our political and governmental processes and result in a more healthy democracy. These ideas are not advanced as cure-alls, but rather illustrate the types of reforms that should be advanced by the reform movement and embraced by independent-minded lawmakers to improve the functioning of our democracy.

1. The February Primary Date Should Be Moved Back to June

Right out of the gate, staring right at us as I write this book, is a major problem that should be addressed: the date of the Illinois primary.

"Did you ever try to pound a yard sign for a candidate into the ground in Illinois in January?" Duane Noland, my fellow IRC commissioner, captured, in one sentence, what is fundamentally wrong with Illinois' decision to retain its February primary and reject a later primary date. Noland, who possesses the quick wit and homespun wisdom of Illinois' heartland, was no stranger to Illinois government and politics. He served honorably in both the Illinois House and Illinois Senate and, in serving, developed a sincere appreciation for public officials and candidates for public office. He does not view members of the legislature as evil or crooked; to the contrary, he believes that members of the legislature and statewide offices come to Springfield to do the right thing.

Conducting a primary in the dead of winter, however, makes no sense. It insults the democratic process by automatically lowering the level of citizen participation. There are a myriad of negatives to the early primary date:

1. Given the cold and probable inclement weather, we all but guarantee a lower turnout;
2. We unfairly force candidates to compete with the holiday season for the public's attention;
3. We hold elections before the commencement of the legislative session and thereby deny voters the right to evaluate the candidates based on the success (or failure) of that legislative session;
4. We dramatically lengthen the general election campaign, which typically is more costly and thus requires greater fundraising. The longer campaign cycle also diverts government officials' focus away from their important job of governing.

In short, a February primary effectively provides

a built-in benefit to the incumbent candidates and detriment to the challengers. It is these "Incumbent Protection Act" provisions that make a fraud-weary citizenry even more cynical and thereby less likely to engage in the political process.

> Conducting a primary in the dead
> of winter makes no sense.

Prior to 2008, Illinois had a mid-March primary. In 2007, in a public nod to Illinois' favorite son, Barack Obama, on his journey to the White House, Illinois moved up its primary in a purported attempt to become more relevant to the presidential election process. Ironically enough, due to the fact that the Obama-Clinton race went well into that summer, the movement of the primary from mid-March to early February provided no meaningful electoral boost to then-candidate Obama. Nevertheless, with the presidential campaign now over, there is simply no persuasive justification to keep the current date, particularly in non-presidential years. It should have been moved forward, but it wasn't. So, as a state that serves as an important barometer on electoral participation in our nation, we've made it harder for citizens to participate during a most critical period in our history. That's cynical and simply wrong.

The fact is that this primary date issue has taken on additional significance in the 2010 election cycle. A good recent sign for our democracy is that for some of the most important, high-profile races—such as governor—we have had hotly contested primaries on both sides of the aisle. No doubt some entrants into these important races were motivated by the desire to answer the call to serve Illinois in a time of need. Yet, by virtue of the legislature's decision to keep the February date, all the candidates who are attempting to distinguish themselves in this critical election cycle are facing obstacles that need not—and should not—ever have been there.

As part of our reform proposals, the IRC pushed for a June primary date, but we received very little support inside the walls of the state Capitol. We were told that there was simply no real support in the legislature for such a measure. Of course not. Those inside state government only saw their own vulnerability if the primary date was moved to a time when more citizens would be more likely to participate in the electoral process. Chalk another one up for the "Incumbent Protection Act."

2. Illinois Should Study and Pursue Mail-In Voting to Enhance Citizen Participation

Given the state of our democracy, I think we should take the electoral participation issue a step further and consider more dramatic proposals to engage our citizens. In that effort, our legislators should think "outside the box" to bring these electoral enhancement proposals to the table.

Legislators should think "outside the box" to bring these electoral enhancement proposals to the table.

One such proposal that merits study and analysis for potential adoption by Illinois is statewide mail-in voting. While a relatively recent phenomenon in the electoral process—it has only been around about 30 years—mail-in voting now decides everything from local elections to presidential elections in certain jurisdictions. The experience of the state of Oregon, which is the only state that has adopted statewide mail-in voting, deserves particular study. Why can't we allow everyone to have this same opportunity to vote without taking time off work or having to go out in bad weather and wait in line to do so? Again, those who want to control the end result will be against any movement in this direction, but what about the rest of us? The truth is that, with the recent adoption of "no-excuse absentee voting," where voters can now vote weeks before the election, we are moving in that direction already. Why not take the next step?

In fact, inspired by the Oregon experience, a pilot project to allow mail-in voting in Illinois was already proposed. In 2009, HB 1113 proposed that mail-in voting be attempted in the 2010 general election in a county selected by the State Board of Elections. HB 1113 was a modest but appropriate proposal that never got very far.

The potential benefits of mail-in voting to Illinois voters are substantial: higher turnout rates; more efficiently managed (and possibly cheaper) elections; and—given the "take home test" nature of mail-in voting—more informed decision-making by voters. For example, voters who want to vote intelligently in elections for judges would have the opportunity to research the judicial candidates' positions and endorsements before casting their ballots at home, without having to bring cumbersome lists into the voting booth, or worse, voting in an uninformed manner.

Of course, the key potential pitfall—the risk of compromising the integrity of the ballot process—

is a serious one that cannot be ignored, especially in Illinois, with our history of voting fraud and ballot manipulation. The Oregon experience has not yielded significant concerns about enhanced ballot manipulation, but Illinois has a more troubled history regarding vote fraud. Accordingly, we need to explore technological protections. For example, a simple bar code on each ballot might allow the voter to trace his or her vote from beginning to end.

Of course, the key potential pitfall cannot be ignored.

The results from Oregon and other jurisdictions that have adopted mail-in voting are hard to ignore. For the last three presidential races, Oregon has had some of the highest voter-participation rates of the 50 states. While Oregon has a history of citizen activism, are Oregonians a fundamentally more engaged group, even than, say, their Pacific Northwest brethren? Unlikely. The most likely distinguishing factor is the ease of ballot access.

As to the concerns of increased risk of ballot integrity issues, clearly much study would need to be done here. However, with the growing usage of the absentee ballot process in Illinois and across the country, the risk of ballot compromise is already upon us. Other issues, such as the potential "poll tax" nature of the mail-in voting process can be addressed in a number of ways, including by providing a number of free, secure drop-off sites.

To be clear, I do not suggest that mail-in voting is some form of panacea, or that it should be adopted immediately without substantial review and study. Further, some current ballot-access experts believe we should focus more on easing voting registration requirements (e.g., to make same-day registration a reality) in order to enhance voter turnout rates. However, I raise mail-in voting and same-day registration as the types of targeted measures that might provide a positive boost to our disaffected electorate—an electorate who needs every reasonable opportunity to participate in the electoral process in easier and more accessible ways.

3. The Legislature Should Permit Bills with Meaningful Support to Get to the Floor

While most of the discussion in this book has been devoted to the merits of reform proposals, based on my IRC experience, a spotlight needs to be shone on the Springfield legislative process—or lack thereof.

Though some may think that the process is simply "inside baseball" stuff that is not important to the ultimate outcome, nothing could be further from the truth. During the 2009 legislative session, two significant pieces of legislation exposed fundamental flaws in this legislative process: the campaign finance reform bill and the Video Gaming Act related to the capital bill. By and large, the key provisions of these important bills were "negotiated" behind closed doors. When final bills were brought to the floor, votes were then taken promptly with little substantive public debate. What alarmed some of us rookie observers of the legislative process was that this appears to be standard operating procedure in Springfield. That is not healthy for democracy but, we were told, it wasn't about to change. Two procedural fixes should be considered, to increase the likelihood we don't replicate the results of the 2009 session:

1. Decreasing the influence of the too-powerful House Rules Committee;
2. Increasing the scrutiny major bills face by requiring substantive testimony and public release of the final bill before votes are taken.

As to the first, during our IRC hearings on government transparency, Illinois State Comptroller Dan

Hynes testified about his frustration with the legislative process. In his brief tutorial on "How Laws Are Made 101," Hynes talked about the powerful function of the House Rules Committee, which serves as the gate-keeping mechanism for a bill on its way to a vote on the floor. He said, "The Rules Committee is where good bills go to die." That is precisely what happened to House Bill 24, a solid piece of campaign finance legislation that imposed meaningful contribution limits on all players. The key provisions of HB 24 were supported by reform groups and were, in fact, quite similar in many respects to the campaign finance bill advanced by the IRC I discussed earlier.

By the end of the legislative session, HB 24 had garnered substantial bipartisan support to the point where over 50% of the *entire* House supported the measure. In a fairly dramatic development by Springfield standards, Democratic Representative Julie Hamos, in an end-of-session speech in support of HB 24, implored her Democratic colleagues not to "follow along like lemmings" to her party leadership's opposition to the bill. Her bold action did not carry the day. Even though HB 24 had enough support to pass the full House if called to a vote on the floor, the bill never got out of the Rules Committee and therefore could not be voted on by the full House or Senate. That's just wrong.

> *Even though HB 24 had enough support to pass the full House if called to a vote on the floor, the bill never got out of the Rules Committee.*

While HB 24 was bottled up in committee, the leadership-sponsored campaign finance bill, House Bill 7, sailed through the process. And what a "process" it was. The final version of HB 7 was negotiated behind closed doors and ultimately released at 2:30 in the morning. That same day, before any meaningful public discussion could take place, the bill was called to a vote in the Senate Executive Committee, and that same evening it was brought to the floor of the full Senate for a vote. Months later, after Governor Quinn reversed course and properly decided to veto HB 7 as inadequate reform, the successor campaign finance bill was again negotiated behind closed doors, albeit with the participation of some reform groups. Yet again, the final bill was released and votes were taken before the public was given any meaningful period to discuss, debate, and potentially refine the provisions. What kind of a democratic "process" is that?

During the same legislative session, similar closed-door tactics were employed to ram through a controversial and significant piece of legislation authorizing a major expansion of video poker to fund a large public works project. The plan was to legalize and greatly increase the number of video poker machines in towns across the state, with proceeds from this gambling being directed to fund a large public works project. While it is not my purpose to focus on the pros and cons of the increased use of gambling proceeds as a funding source or to criticize the underlying merits of the public works project, the legislative path for this bill and its recent aftermath provides another example of the critical need for a meaningful legislative process.

With virtually no public debate in Springfield regarding the underlying financial assumptions or the long-term law enforcement and regulatory consequences of expanding this form of gambling, the bill lurched through the General Assembly in the end-of-session madness in Springfield. A prominent member of the House, Democratic Representative Jack Franks, publicly complained about the process: "The legislation creating the Video Gaming Act was rushed through the General Assembly in

111

only two days. As a result, legislators were not given the opportunity to discuss this important issue with their constituents, on whose behalf they cast their votes. Illinois citizens are the people who will be most affected by this expansion, and they should be given the right to weigh in on it." Nor did we have a chance to analyze how comparable bills in other states had fared after they were passed. If we had, we would have seen that some of these bills have not met their hype from a revenue-generation standpoint. But we didn't take time to talk about it.

After the public works project bill was passed with video poker as a key funding source, the failings of the process were revealed and provided, perhaps, a bit of a silver lining for the reform movement. The bill permitted communities to "opt out" of video poker by local referendum. In the weeks and months following passage, a slew of towns in Illinois—to the surprise and consternation of those who rammed the bill through—have said "thanks but no thanks" to expanded video poker.

From a revenue perspective, every town or governmental entity that says no—and there have been over 50 to date and the number is growing—reduces the anticipated revenue stream to fund the public works project.

So, even if democracy wins, it loses, all because of the desire of insiders to avoid free and open debate on such an important issue.

Even if democracy wins, it loses.

The current use of the committee system and be-hind-closed-doors dealmaking has had a significant effect on efforts to pass all kinds of important legislation. In a democracy, it should not be difficult to get bills with broad-based support to the floor of the legislature (like HB 24), nor should it be easy to pass bills (like the Video Gaming Act) from both chambers with little public vetting.

So what's to be done? As we proposed in the IRC process, the House and Senate should adopt rules requiring that each bill introduced to the House Rules Committee or its Senate equivalent, the Assignment Committee, be subject to a full committee vote if the bill has a threshold level of support. I would add a requirement that the lower threshold needs to include at least one member from the majority party to avoid minority party manipulation of the process.

The naysayers say that the internal rules of the

House will never change because Speaker Madigan won't let them. Of course, they are right for now. The internal rules will not change without a transformation in the mindset of rank-and-file legislators, particularly those in the House of Representatives, where Speaker Madigan wields virtually exclusive control.

Yet we have seen some positive changes in the Senate recently on the gate-keeping committees, and it is up to House members to show their constituents they want to improve our democracy. They have another chance this spring to show us they want to do better.

As to the second issue, significant bills such as a multi-billion-dollar public works project with video poker expansion should have substantive public hearings and a period between public release of the bill and a vote. We need public testimony on major pieces of legislation, as well as a meaningful period for the public and legislators to read and comment on the language of significant bills, *before* the vote. How is this unreasonable when we are talking about fundamentally altering legalized gambling in our state? We must give more than lip service to democratic principles to avoid legislative train wrecks like we now have with the video poker debacle.

4. Technology Should Be Utilized to Enhance FOIA and, Ultimately, Make It Obsolete

"Sunlight is said to be the best of disinfectants." Those oft-quoted words of a legendary Supreme Court justice almost 100 years ago have particular application in Illinois today. Indeed, there is a pretty good argument that more transparency throughout Illinois government is the best first step to exposing, and thereby improving, the political culture of our state. In fact, as noted earlier one of the tangible reforms emanating from the 2009 legislative session was the bolstering of key provisions of Illinois' Freedom of Information Act, the so-called FOIA. These measures, and the ultimate bill, were advanced by Attorney General Lisa Madigan, with an assist by the IRC and other reform groups. But that was just a start.

The truth of the matter is that government has done far too little to harness the tremendous benefits of technological advancement to shed light on the democratic process. Actually, the ultimate goal of the effort to make government more transparent should be, in effect, to make FOIA obsolete. That is, instead of citizens submitting a written request to a state agency like the Illinois Department of

115

Transportation to obtain information on a construction contract, that information should be posted or otherwise available online so that the request never has to be made. After all, citizens shouldn't have to ask in order to find out what their government is doing. As we learned and heard during the IRC process, injecting government with a sense of institutional transparency will take time. Further, the transition to an on-line world may, in many cases, require substantial upfront costs. Such costs may be particularly steep in these tough budget times, but government leaders and respective agency heads should push to make incremental transitions to a more transparent democracy. For a democracy that is not transparent is no democracy at all.

Conclusion: What We Can Do Right Now

In putting together the Illinois Reform Commission (IRC), I was honored to be joined by members who proudly had engaged the political culture. In addition to those I've already mentioned, there were members like Lawrence Oliver, a former federal prosecutor and someone who fought to hold Governor Blagojevich's Administration accountable as a member of the Executive Ethics Commission. I was also proud to work alongside Sheila Simon, an accomplished attorney and law school professor in southern Illinois, who is carrying on the tradition of her father, the great statesman and beloved Illinois Senator, Paul Simon.

I was equally honored to be joined by talented citizens who were not steeped in political experience: folks like Pat Fitzgerald, the Northwestern college football coach; Kate Maehr, the executive director of one of the most respected charitable organizations in the Chicagoland area; Tasha Green, the executive director of an organization who works with inner-city high school youth; Fr. Dennis Holtschneider, president of DePaul University; and Doug Johnson, a neurologist who volunteered to serve as a medic on the battlefields of Iraq.

All made important contributions to our overall product. Their efforts confirmed and reinforced a critical truth about government: We will have a much better government when we bring the outside, common sense voices of citizens inside the process. At the end of the IRC process, I had two fundamental takeaways:

1. Most insiders will resist any fundamental change because they have benefited from the system they have built;
2. If fundamental change is to occur, we citizens have to *earn* it.

In that spirit, I am often asked by those who want to engage the political process further what they can do to get involved. So many of us live hectic lives and are appropriately focused on family and work or school. If we do want to contribute, however, there are many ways to help, and most of them aren't always time-intensive.

Of course, our participation should start with two time-honored traditions:

1. **Voting.** While the current situation of the February primary in Illinois makes voting more difficult, and there can be appropriate reluctance to declare one's party affiliation, if we want to effect change, we simply can't use that as an excuse not to cast our ballots now and in every future election.

2. **Contacting our public officials.** During the IRC process many sophisticated observers told me that when a politician gets four or five emails on one topic, he or she thinks a revolution is afoot. While that may be a bit of an overstatement, the point is a good one. If enough people let their voices be heard, public officials will listen.

If we have time for something more:

1. **We can sign or circulate petitions.** As I noted earlier, I believe redistricting reform is an important, achievable objective. Go to www.ilfairmap.

119

com, download a petition and help get the signatures needed by May 2, 2010, to put this needed reform on the ballot.

2. **We can apply for appointment to a state board or commission.** Recently, Governor Quinn has created an on-line application process at www.appointments.il.gov. To his credit, the governor has reached outside the typical process to seek new people to get involved in government, and he should continue to do that.

3. **We can join a reform group.** One of my most pleasant experiences as chair of the IRC was meeting so many smart and dedicated people. One of the most impressive umbrella organizations I saw was Change Illinois. Another wonderful grassroots organization was United Power for Action and Justice. I'm currently on the board of the Better Government Association, which has recently reasserted its place as a strong, non-partisan watchdog organization. All of these groups— and many others—would love to have more people become engaged.

4. **We can write short letters to the editor.** You'd be amazed how often they will print what you have to say.

5. **We can submit Freedom of Information Act**

requests. When we think we see something fishy, we should inquire about it.

6. **We can attend village hall, school board or local government meetings.** When we monitor how they are run and observe whether there is transparency in the effort, we hold our government's feet to the fire.

7. **We can donate funds to our favorite candidates.** While I have criticized the pay-to-play culture, I want to emphasize that showing our support of a candidate through a financial contribution is an important right we all have. Many candidates, even those running for the highest office, appreciate the smaller donations, as they help a candidate establish a broad base of support. It will also be refreshing for candidates to know that all we demand in return for our donations is their honorable service.

8. **We can encourage good people to run for office.** If we bring more candidates who support the reform agenda into the political system, and support those who already do, perhaps we can make change occur more quickly. Of course, this option is not for everyone and requires enormous personal and family sacrifice.

These ideas are merely some examples of what we citizens can do to reform how politics is done in Illinois. These efforts will not work every time, and change will *not* occur overnight, but that's okay, as long as we make tangible progress and do not use the enormity of the task as an excuse for inaction.

We need to put together victory after victory, small and large, to move us to a better place in Illinois.

We need to put together victory after victory.

While much of what I have proposed in this book requires changes in the law, we all should understand that the key elements to changing the culture of corruption are not to be found in any law book or new statute. The change in the law will only happen when we citizens have changed our own attitudes and expectations about what kind of government we deserve. Indeed, this is the core challenge: to change people's attitudes and expectations about their government.

In the passionate pursuit of this effort, we will, of course, need public officials who are able, courageous, and willing to expend political capital on these issues. We will also need government leaders to advance bold, responsible, and thoughtful initiatives; to take on special interests; and to honor our democratic system.

Most of all, we will need everyday citizens to take up the mission—day in and day out—to challenge the culture of corruption.

Acknowledgments

In writing this book, I am indebted to each of my fellow Illinois Reform Commission (IRC) members: Anita Alvarez, Cook County State's Attorney; Pamela Davis, CEO Edward Hospital; Pat Fitzgerald, Northwestern University football coach; Hanke Gratteau, former Managing Editor, News, Chicago Tribune; Tasha Green, Executive Director, High Jump; David Hoffman, former City of Chicago Inspector General; Rev. Dennis Holtschneider, President, DePaul University; Douglas Johnson, Neurosurgeon; Kate Maehr, Executive Director, Chicago Food Depository; Brad McMillan, Institute for Principled Leadership, Bradley University; N. Duane Noland, President and CEO, Association of Illinois Electrical Cooperatives; Lawrence Oliver, Chief Counsel Investigations, Boeing Company;

Sheila Simon, Professor of Law, Southern Illinois University; and Rev. Scott Willis, former Pastor, Parkwood Baptist Church. Due to your dedication and commitment, I thoroughly enjoyed and was heartened by the IRC journey. Thank you for your service.

I would like to acknowledge my colleagues at Perkins Coie, led by Chicago managing partner, Chris Wilson, and firm managing partner, Robert Giles, who supported my firm's investment in the IRC's efforts. I am also grateful for the many partners, associates, paralegals, and assistants in our Chicago office who participated in the IRC work. Special thanks to my assistant, Amber Norris, for her tireless commitment to the IRC and my assistant, Dorothy Gallagher, for her review and support of this book; and associate Jade Lambert, for her review and insightful comments.

I am grateful for the dedication and honor demonstrated by the members of the Operation Safe Road investigative team, including Assistant U.S. Attorneys Zach Fardon, Joel Levin, and Laurie Barsella; FBI agents Ray Ruebenson, Vick Lombardo and Ken Samuel; United States Postal Inspector Basil Demczak; IRS Agents Shari Schindler, Sue Roderick and Mark Lischka; United States Department of

Transportation Agents David Hoeffler and Kevin Shirley; paralegal Sharon Getty; secretary Barbara Buckner and Secretary of State investigators Russ Sonneveld, Ed Hammer, and Don Strom.

I am grateful for the inspiration provided by my friend, the recently departed Carlos Hernandez Gomez. A Chicago original, he fought the fight against the culture of corruption as an objective journalist with an encyclopedic knowledge of the political game and its players. In his final days, I discussed this book with him and he was very supportive. He will always be remembered.

I appreciate the unwavering support of former U.S. Attorney Scott Lassar, who built and supported the Safe Road team and his successor, Patrick Fitzgerald, the best U.S. Attorney this district has ever had. A special thanks to my close friend, Zach Fardon, for his personal sacrifice for the Safe Road team and for his efforts in reviewing and commenting on this book.

I was honored to work alongside dozens of dedicated men and women in federal law enforcement in my twelve years at the U.S. Attorney's office. Thank you to Tom Durkin and Mike Shepard for giving me an opportunity as an intern; former U.S. Attorney Jim Burns for hiring me; Scott Levine for teaching me how to conduct a public corruption investigation; and the many dedicated agents and employees of the FBI, the U.S. Postal Service, the Department of Labor, and other state and federal agencies for making our work possible. They received little praise but are true unsung heroes.

A special thank you to Greg Pierce and his team at ACTA Publications for encouraging me to write this book, keeping me on schedule, and providing editing, technical support, and encouragement along the way. Special thanks to Jim McGowan for exhibiting the patience of Job in addressing the myriad drafts of the book.

I am grateful to my law school classmate and talented friend, Eric Adelstein, who provided helpful ideas and comments for this book and captured the essence of Illinois' culture of corruption in a video he created and donated to the IRC.

Last but certainly not least, I am forever indebted to my mother and father, Rosemarie and John Collins, for their unconditional love and support. I am also grateful for the support of my six siblings, who have encouraged and supported me as an adult (after some early childhood torture). Special thanks to my older brother and mentor, Shawn Collins, who taught me many life lessons and gave assistance in writing this book.